| DATE DUE | | | |
|---|---|---|---|
|  |  |  |  |
|  |  |  |  |
|  |  |  |  |
|  |  |  |  |
|  |  |  |  |
|  |  |  |  |
|  |  |  |  |
|  |  |  |  |
|  |  |  |  |
|  |  |  |  |
|  |  |  |  |
|  |  |  |  |
|  |  |  |  |
|  |  |  |  |
|  |  |  |  |

# OCTOPUSES

# OCTOPUSES

## JENNY MARKERT

THE CHILD'S WORLD

**PHOTO CREDITS**
Norbert Wu: front cover, back cover,
2, 6, 9, 10, 13, 20, 21, 23, 27, 28, 31
Marty Snyderman: 15, 16, 19, 24

Distributed to schools and libraries in the United States by
ENCYCLOPAEDIA BRITANNICA EDUCATIONAL CORP.
310 South Michigan Avenue
Chicago, Illinois  60604

Library of Congress Cataloging-in-Publication Data
Markert, Jenny.
Octopuses / by Jenny Markert.
p.   cm.
Summary:  Introduces the physical and  behavioral
characteristics of octopuses.
ISBN 0-89565-836-4
1. Octopuses--Juvenile literature.   [1. Octopus.]   I. Title.
QL430.3.02M37   1992                               91-37720
594'.56--dc20                                            CIP
                                                              AC

*For Lis and Duke*

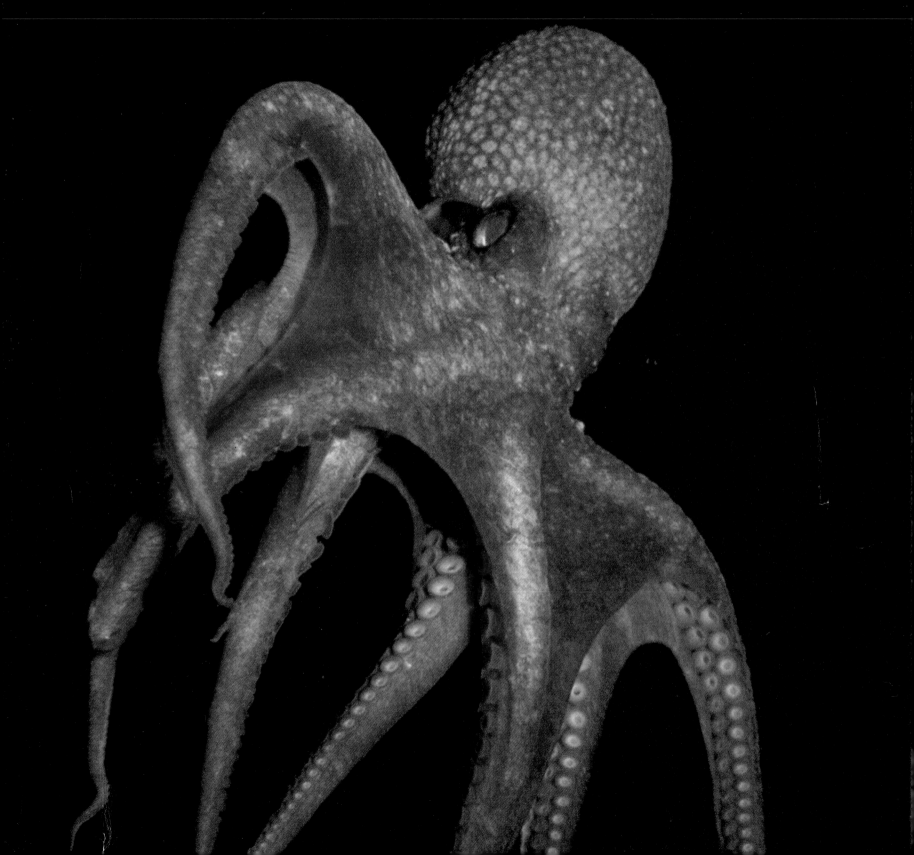

From the surface of the sea, it's hard to tell what kinds of animals lurk below. Many people think that slimy and horrible creatures live in the ocean. The octopus is one sea creature that seems to have this reputation. Octopuses are often thought of as creepy monsters with glaring eyes and coiling arms. Some people think that an octopus will strangle the life out of anything it sees.

Despite what people imagine, octopuses are actually shy, harmless animals. They would rather sneak away than attack a person. Octopuses are feared mainly because of their unusual appearance. An octopus's body is much different from yours. An octopus does not have a skeleton. It has a boneless body and a very small head. In this picture, the baglike thing on the right is the octopus's body. The animal's eyes stick up on top of its head. An octopus can see backward without turning its head!

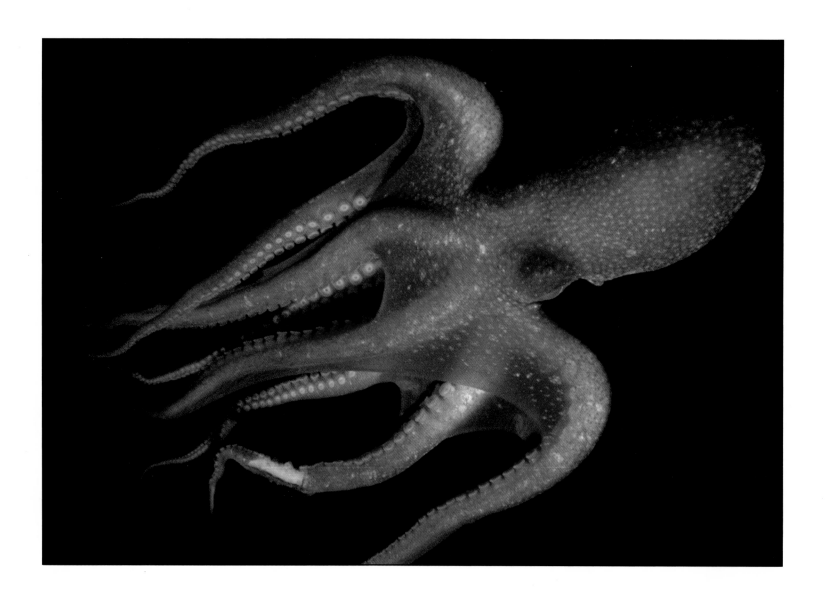

The octopus's most striking feature is its eight arms, or *tentacles*. The word *octopus* means "eight-armed one." Strangely enough, an octopus's arms are attached to its head, not its body. The tentacles are long and muscular. They can coil and twist in any direction. Under each tentacle are rows of little suction cups. Most octopuses have more than 200 suction cups on each arm. These cups help octopuses cling to rocky walls and catch food.

There are about 150 different kinds of octopuses. They live throughout the world's oceans, from warm coral reefs to the frozen seas of Antarctica. Most octopuses live in shallow water. One type of octopus lives two miles beneath the ocean surface.

Octopuses vary greatly in size. Common octopuses are about the size of a skateboard. However, the largest octopuses grow as long as a school bus. The octopus in this picture is one of the smallest. It is slightly longer than your thumb and weighs about the same as a peanut!

Regardless of their size, octopuses are very shy and secretive. They prefer to live alone. Octopuses make homes in rocky caves, reef crevices, and wrecked ships. Small octopuses may live in vacant seashells or human pollution, like pop bottles or tin cans. They leave their dens only to avoid a nosey enemy or to find food.

Finding food is easy for octopuses; many creatures are tasty to them. Sometimes an octopus collects a pile of oysters or clams. The octopus uses its suction cups to pull the shells apart and get the food inside.

Octopuses also eat crabs and lobsters. The octopus in this picture has just captured a crab. If you look closely, you can see the crab's claw. The octopus will bite through the crab's shell and kill the animal with a dose of poison. The poison also softens the crab's flesh so the octopus can suck up its meal.

Octopuses also have ways to catch faster prey. From its home or hiding place, an octopus can bolt out and grab passing fish. Octopuses are fast swimmers and can dart back and forth in any direction. Beneath an octopus's head is a pouch called a *mantle*. When the octopus wants to swim forward, its mantle swells up like a water balloon. Then strong muscles push the water out through a special tube called a *spiracle*. The rushing water pushes the octopus forward like a rocket.

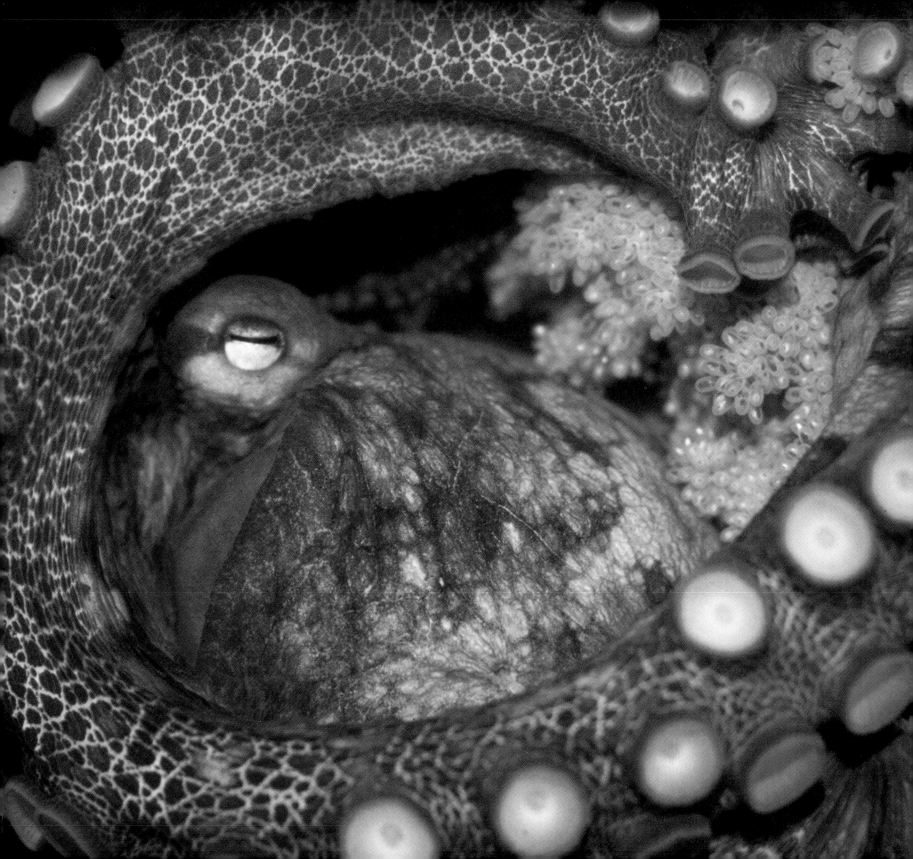

Besides using their dens to ambush passing fish, female octopuses use their homes to raise their young. When a female octopus is about four years old, she lays thousands of eggs,

sometimes even 200,000 or more. She strings the eggs along the walls of her home. Each egg is about the size and shape of a grain of rice. After all the eggs are laid, the female octopus stays nearby, protecting and cleaning them.

The tiny eggs hatch after a month or so. The mother octopus dies about five days later, leaving her babies to care for themselves. From the moment they are born, baby octopuses are faced with danger. They are no bigger than fleas and cannot swim. They drift in the ocean, hoping to avoid hungry sea creatures. Most of the baby octopuses are not so lucky. Only a few survive until their first birthday.

Even after they are full grown, octopuses still face many dangers. Large-mouthed fish, seals, and moray eels like to eat octopuses. Luckily, mature octopuses are great escape artists. One way they trick their enemies is through camouflage. Octopuses are commonly white with red or gray dots. Next to coral or rocky sea bottoms, they are very hard to see.

If an enemy does spot an octopus, the octopus can actually change colors! A whole wave of different colors may flow across its skin. The octopus can turn red, green, or even black. The octopus's skin also can change patterns, showing stripes, solids, or dots.

Scientists think that octopuses also change colors to show their moods. Frightened octopuses turn pale, light colors. Angry octopuses are solid purple or black. When they eat, octopuses are often covered with spots and blotches.

If the octopus's show of colors doesn't confuse its enemy, the octopus is not yet doomed. Instead of sticking around to fight, it tries to make a clever escape. When the enemy attacks, the octopus squirts a dark, inklike liquid into the water. The ink cloud looks and smells like the octopus. When the enemy attacks, it finds only an inky blob. Meanwhile, the octopus darts away to safety.

Although they live beneath the ocean in hidden caves and sunken ships, octopuses are not the monsters we imagine them to be. Octopuses are shy, harmless animals that would rather flee from an enemy than fight. They have many clever ways to avoid danger and capture food. Octopuses force us to rethink our old ideas about the creepy monsters we thought roamed the seas.

# THE CHILD'S WORLD
# NATUREBOOKS

## Wildlife Library

## Space Library

## Adventure Library